HELEN HALL LIBR,
City of League Cit
100 West Walker
League City, TX 77573

DISCA

DEC 1 5

DISCARD

People Who Help

A KIDS' GUIDE TO COMMUNITY HEROES

by Rachelle Kreisman
with illustrations by Tim Haggerty

RED
CHAIR
·PRESS·

HELEN HALL LIBRARY
100 Walker St
League City, TX 77573

DISCARD

Please visit our website at **www.redchairpress.com** for more high-quality products for young readers.

Special thanks to our community heroes. Police Department of Egremont, MA Fire Department of Great Barrington, MA.

Publisher's Cataloging-In-Publication Data
(Prepared by The Donohue Group, Inc.)

Kreisman, Rachelle.
    People who help : a kids' guide to community heroes / by Rachelle Kreisman ; with illustrations by Tim Haggerty. -- [First edition].

    pages : illustrations ; cm. -- (Start smart: community)

    Summary: Heroes are all around us: people who help others stay safe and well, and protect our homes and businesses. Includes fun facts.
    Interest age level: 006-009.
    Edition statement supplied by publisher.
    Includes index.
    Issued also as an ebook.
    ISBN: 978-1-939656-89-6 (library hardcover)
    ISBN: 978-1-939656-90-2 (paperback)

    1. Community life--Juvenile literature. 2. Public safety--Juvenile literature. 3. Medical personnel--Juvenile literature. 4. Refuse collectors--Juvenile literature. 5. School crossing guards--Juvenile literature. 6. Community life. 7. Public safety. 8. Medical personnel. 9. Refuse collectors. 10. School crossing guards. I. Haggerty, Tim. II. Title.

HM761 .K741 2015
307   2014957484

Copyright © 2016 Red Chair Press LLC

All rights reserved. No part of this book may be reproduced, stored in an information or retrieval system, or transmitted in any form by any means, electronic, mechanical including photocopying, recording, or otherwise without the prior written permission from the Publisher. For permissions, contact info@redchairpress.com

Illustration credits: p. 1, 5, 7, 8, 9, 10, 11, 12, 17, 19, 20, 24, 26, 27, 29, 32: Tim Haggerty

Photo credits: Cover p. 1, 6, 7, 10, 11, 27, 30: Marisa Burntitus for RCP; p. 4, 12, 20, 31, 25: Dreamstime; p. 5 (left, center, right), 8, 9, 13, 15, 16, 17, 18, 19, 20, 21, 22, 23, 26: Shutterstock; p. 32: Courtesy of the author, Rachelle Kreisman

This series first published by:
Red Chair Press LLC   PO Box 333   South Egremont, MA 01258-0333

Printed in the United States of America

042015 1P WRZF15

Table of Contents

Words in **bold type** are defined in the glossary.

CHAPTER 1

Community Life

Did you know that you are part of a community? A **community** is a place where people live, work, and play. It is made up of neighborhoods. Those neighborhoods are made up of families.

Three kinds of communities are urban, suburban, and rural. **Urban areas** are cities with tall buildings and many people. **Suburban areas** are near cities. People often live in houses and small apartments. **Rural areas** have fewer people and more land. Farms are often found there. Think about your community. Do you live in an urban, suburban, or rural place?

🏠 Communities can be large cities or small towns.

People in a community have many kinds of jobs. Some people work to help others. They are community helpers. They include police officers, firefighters, and doctors, just to name a few. Would you like to learn more? Keep reading to get the scoop on jobs that helpers do.

JUST JOKING!

Q: What runs through neighborhoods, but does not move?

A: Roads!

CHAPTER 2

Police Officers

Police officers protect people and their **property.** The officers make sure people follow laws. Laws are rules made by the government to keep order.

Each police officer has a certain area to patrol. The officer checks the area to make sure it is safe. Most officers travel in police cars. The cars have flashing lights and sirens. They alert people that police are coming.

Flashing lights and sirens tell people help is on the way.

🏠 A police officer inspects an accident.

Police officers are quick to arrive during an emergency. How do they know where to go? People call 9-1-1. The operator contacts the officers to tell them the details.

Was there a car accident? Police race to the scene. They talk to people and study the accident. Officers try to figure out what happened. If anyone was hurt, the officers can perform first aid.

FUN FACT

Officers may also patrol areas by motorcycle, bicycle, boat, helicopter, and snowmobile. Some officers even ride horses.

Police officers rush to crime scenes. They study clues and record facts. If they catch a criminal, officers can arrest that person. Is someone trying to rob a business or steal a car? Police officers are on their way!

Some officers control traffic. They make sure people are driving safely. Is someone driving too fast? An officer can pull the driver over. Then the officer may give that person a speeding ticket.

DID YOU KNOW?

Not all police officers use cars with lights. In many places officers even get around on a 2-wheeled personal scooter, called Segway.

Each day for a police officer is different. Anything can happen. One day, an officer may have to control a large crowd. Another day, he or she may need to stop a fight or help a lost child.

To be a police officer, you must be fit and strong. Officers must be able to defend themselves and others. They may also have to chase after criminals to put handcuffs on them. Whatever the day brings, police officers are ready!

JUST JOKING!

Q: What did the jacket say to the police officer?

A: Don't worry—I've got you covered!

In many communities, police use bikes to patrol.

CHAPTER 3

Firefighters

You hear sirens and see flashing lights. That's not a police car though. It is a fire truck! Cars move over as firefighters speed to an emergency. Firefighters are trained to put out fires. They also rescue people and animals.

Firefighters help in other ways, too. They treat sick and injured people by giving them first aid. When disasters strike, firefighters are called to the scene. They work to save people in danger. Was an area hit by an earthquake or a flood? Here come the firefighters!

FUN FACT

Most fire trucks are red, but they don't have to be! Some communities have chosen other colors. Their trucks come in yellow, orange, green, blue, black, and purple.

Firefighters have a dangerous job. To stay safe, they wear special gear. It protects them from heat, flames, and smoke. The gear includes a helmet, a jacket, gloves, pants, and boots. Firefighters also wear a mask and a breathing tank.

Some firefighters stay overnight at a fire station. They eat and sleep there. When the alarm sounds, they put on their gear. Then they rush to the fire truck. After a fire, firefighters clean their gear and the truck.

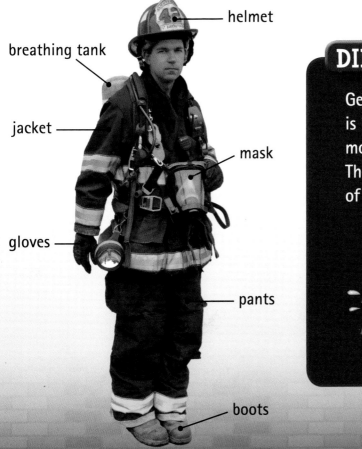

helmet

breathing tank

jacket

mask

gloves

pants

boots

DID YOU KNOW?

Gear worn by firefighters is heavy. It can weigh more than 60 pounds! That is about the weight of 7 gallons of water.

What do firefighters do when they are not fighting fires? They learn new skills and take part in practice drills. They check the equipment to make sure it is in working order. Firefighters exercise to keep active.

And that's not all. Firefighters also visit schools to teach fire safety. They want kids to know what to do in case of a fire and how to prevent fires.

TRY THIS!

Every family needs a fire escape plan. Walk through your home and find two ways out of each room. Those ways can be doors or windows. Choose a place outside where everyone can meet. Draw a picture of the plan and talk about it with your family. Then practice the plan together to make sure you are prepared. In the event of a fire, get out quickly and stay out!

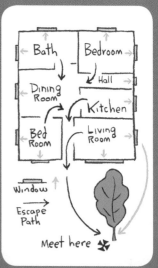

To become a firefighter, you need to be fit and brave. Firefighters have to be able to lift heavy equipment and carry people from burning buildings.

New firefighters often spend many weeks training. They learn how to use ladders, axes, hoses, and other tools. Spray from a hose can be powerful. It may take several people to aim the spray in the right direction. Firefighters practice working together as a team.

CHAPTER 4

Doctors and Nurses

Doctors and nurses help people stay healthy. When you go for a checkup, you may see a nurse first. He or she may check your height and weight. The nurse might also measure your **blood pressure.** That shows how hard your heart is working to pump blood.

Then the doctor will examine you. If you are sick or hurt, the doctor will try to help you get well again. He or she may give you an order for medicine.

DID YOU KNOW?

Most nurses wear uniforms called scrubs. Scrubs are comfortable and easy to keep clean from germs.

X-rays help doctors see inside the body.

Many different kinds of doctors help people. A **pediatrician** is a doctor who treats kids. Do you have an ear infection? You may need to see an ENT (ear, nose, and throat) doctor. Do cats make you sneeze? Achoo! An allergist (allergy doctor) may be able to help you.

Not every doctor sees patients. Another kind of doctor studies **X-rays** and other scans. He or she gives the results to a patient's doctor.

Doctors and nurses use many kinds of tools. A **stethoscope** lets them listen to your heart and lungs. An **otoscope** gives a look into your ears and nose. A rubber hammer is another tool. It checks your **reflexes.** The doctor will often tap your knee with it. Your leg should kick up on its own!

🏠 Nurses and doctors have many tools to help keep you healthy.

Are you interested in being a doctor or a nurse? You must be curious and like science. Doctors go to school for a long time. After college, they go to medical school for four years. Then they spend several years training. Nurses often go to college for four years.

Doctors and nurses never stop learning. They take classes throughout their careers. They learn new ways to help patients stay healthy.

JUST JOKING!

Q: Why did the teddy bear go to the doctor?

A: It was feeling stuffed up!

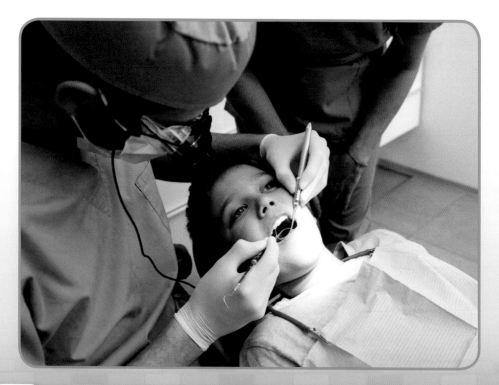

CHAPTER 5

Dentists and Hygienists

Say cheese! Healthy teeth give you a great smile. Dentists and hygienists help people take care of their teeth. During a checkup, you will often see the hygienist first. He or she will clean your teeth.

The hygienist wears rubber gloves, a face mask, and scrubs. That helps keep germs from spreading. Dentists wear gloves and face masks too. They may also wear scrubs or lab coats.

The hygienist will use a tooth scraper to remove **plaque**. That is a sticky film on teeth. It can cause **cavities.** A cavity is a hole in a tooth. Then the hygienist will polish and floss your teeth. He or she may take X-rays of your teeth as well.

JUST JOKING!

Q: What time should you go to the dentist?

A: Tooth-hurty!

You may also have a **fluoride** treatment. Fluoride is a mineral. It helps prevent cavities. You often get to pick a flavor. Bubble gum or cherry, please!

♦ X-rays help a dentist see inside your teeth and gums.

Now your teeth are clean. Nice! It's time to see the dentist. He or she will check your teeth and gums to make sure they are healthy. The dentist will also read any X-rays to see if you have a cavity.

If you have a cavity, the dentist will fix it. But you will most likely have to come back another day. At that time, the dentist will give you a tiny shot to numb the area. Then he or she will clean and fill the cavity. Now you are good to go.

TRY THIS!

Brush your teeth at least twice a day to prevent cavities. Not so fast though! Cleaning your teeth takes time. Set a timer for two to three minutes to get the job done right!

Some dentists have special training. Are your teeth crooked? You may need to see an **orthodontist.** That kind of dentist works to make teeth straight. Other dentists treat gum problems and perform surgery.

How do you become a dentist or hygienist? You must like science and learning. After college, most dentists go to school for four more years. A dentist who wants special training will go to school longer. Hygienists often need to go to college for two years.

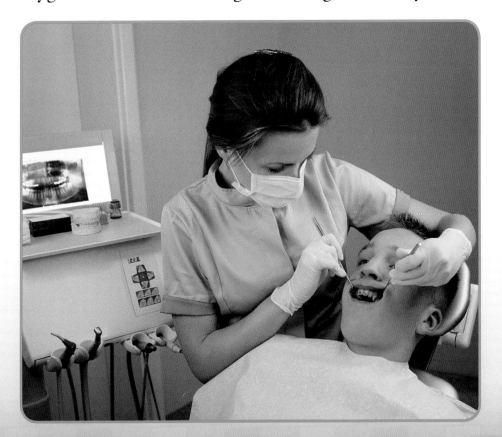

CHAPTER 6

Trash Collectors

Trash collectors help keep our communities clean. They often work in pairs. One person drives a garbage truck. The other person rides on the back. He or she lifts the trash and dumps it into the truck. If the truck has a lift, the worker attaches it to the trash container. The driver operates the lift to pick up the trash and empty it.

Some garbage trucks have a robotic arm. One person drives and operates the arm. It lifts the trash container and empties it. Then the arm places the container back on the ground.

FUN FACT

Americans throw out more than 200 million tons of trash each year. Most cars weigh about a half-ton, or 1,000 pounds. That's a LOT OF TRASH!

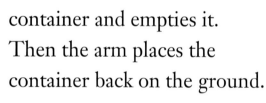

What does it take to be a trash collector? You must like being outdoors and not mind getting dirty. You need to be strong so you can lift heavy objects. Lastly, only early birds need apply. Most trash pick-up starts early in the morning.

To stay safe, trash collectors wear work gloves and boots. They also wear bright-colored clothing. That makes it easy for other drivers to see them.

DID YOU KNOW?

Most trash is taken to a landfill. That is a place where trash is buried. Materials to be recycled are taken to a recycling center. There, the items are sorted and loaded onto a truck. They are taken to factories that use recycled materials to make new products.

CHAPTER 7

Crossing Guards

How do you get to and from school? Some boys and girls walk. Crossing guards help those kids cross streets safely. The guard wears a bright-colored vest. He or she stands near a crosswalk. Some streets have a light that shows when to walk. The guard waits for the light and tells the kids when to cross.

JUST JOKING!

Q: Why did the chicken cross the road?

A: The crossing guard said it was safe!

The crossing guard can control traffic too. He or she holds up a stop sign and walks into the street. All drivers must come to a stop. The kids can now cross safely.

What happens if a driver does not stop? The crossing guard can write down the driver's license plate number. Then the guard can tell school officials and the police.

Being a crossing guard is a part-time job. But it is an important one. In order to keep kids safe, crossing guards must be able to make good decisions. They need to pay careful attention to the kids, traffic lights, and drivers.

CHAPTER 8

Thank You, Helpers!

Wow! Community helpers do so many different jobs. From police officer to crossing guard, each helper plays a big role. How do you know? Just imagine if there were no helpers. Without dentists, people could lose their teeth. Yikes! Without trash collectors, we could have very messy (and stinky) neighborhoods.

No doctors or nurses to keep us healthy? No firefighters to put out fires? You get the idea. A community without helpers would be a terrible place indeed.

The next time you meet a community helper, think about all the work they do. You could even say, "Thank you for your help!" When you grow up, you might want to be a community helper too.

TRY THIS!

Each community has many kinds of helpers. Can you name any other helpers in your community? (Here are two hints to get started: Who delivers your mail? Who teaches you new things?)

Glossary

blood pressure: a measure of how hard your heart is working to pump blood

cavities: holes in teeth

community: cities and towns where people live, work, and play

fluoride: a mineral that helps prevent cavities

orthodontist: a dentist who is trained to make teeth straight

otoscope: a medical tool used to look into a patient's ears and nose

pediatrician: a doctor who treats kids

plaque: a sticky film on teeth that can cause cavities

property: things that belong to someone

reflexes: the body's quick movements in response to something

rural area: an area in the country

scrubs: uniforms worn by medical and dental workers

stethoscope: a medical tool used to listen to a patient's heart and lungs

suburban area: an area near a city

urban area: a city

X-rays: special pictures that show the inside of the body

What Did You Learn?

See how much you learned about community helpers. Answer *true* or *false* for each statement below. Write your answers on a separate piece of paper.

1 A community is made up of neighborhoods.
True or false?

2 Fire trucks are always painted red.
True or false?

3 Police officers are trained to perform first aid.
True or false?

4 Hygienists work to keep people's teeth clean.
True or false?

5 Trash collectors carry stop signs to direct traffic.
True or false?

Answers: 1. True, 2. False (Fire trucks can be red, yellow, orange, green, blue, black, and purple.) 3. True, 4. True, 5. False (Crossing guards, not trash collectors, carry stop signs to direct traffic.)

For More Information

Books

Adamson, Heather. *A Day in the Life of a Firefighter.* Capstone Press, 2004.

Bourgeois, Paulette. *Police Officers.* Fitzgerald Books, 2007.

Bridges, Sarah. *I Drive a Garbage Truck.* Picture Window Books, 2005.

Fluet, Connie. *A Day in the Life of a Nurse.* Capstone Press, 2005.

Heos, Bridget. *Let's Meet a Doctor.* Millbrook Press, 2013.

Kalman, Bobbie. *What is a Community from A to Z?* Crabtree Publishing Company, 2000.

Piehl, Janet. *Sanitation Workers.* Lerner Publishing, 2006.

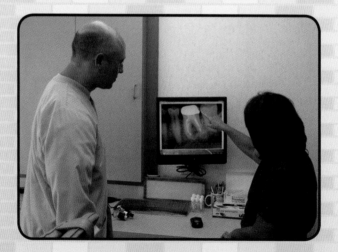

Web Sites

Ben's Guide to U.S. Government for Kids
http://bensguide.gpo.gov/k-2/neighborhood

FEMA Ready Campaign: Home Fires
http://www.ready.gov/kids/know-the-facts/home-fires

KidsHealth: Staying Safe
http://kidshealth.org/kid/watch

University of Washington Medicine: Youth Activities
http://www.uwmedicine.org/education/md-program/admissions/youth/be-a-doctor

ADA: Mouth Healthy Kids
http://www.mouthhealthykids.org

Note to educators and parents: Our editors have carefully reviewed these web sites to ensure they are suitable for children. Web sites change frequently, however, and we cannot guarantee that a site's future contents will continue to meet our high standards of quality and educational value. You may wish to preview these sites and closely supervise children whenever they access the Internet.

Index

About the Author

Rachelle Kreisman has been a children's writer and editor for many years. She is the author of several children's books and hundreds of *Weekly Reader* classroom magazines. When Rachelle is not writing, she enjoys going to places in her community. She likes taking walks, hiking, biking, kayaking, and doing yoga.